AMBASSADORS
TO THE WORLD

AMBASSADORS TO THE WORLD

Declaring God's love

Chris Wright

inter-varsity press

INTER-VARSITY PRESS
38 De Montfort Street, Leicester LE1 7GP, England

First published 1998

British Library Cataloguing in Publication Data
A catalogue record for this book is available from the British
Library

ISBN 0–85110–895–4

Set in Stempel Garamond

Typeset in Great Britain by Parker Typesetting Service, Leicester
Printed in Great Britain by Cox & Wyman Ltd, Reading

*Inter-Varsity Press is the book-publishing division of the
Universities and Colleges Christian Fellowship (formerly the
Inter-Varsity Fellowship), a student movement linking Christian
Unions in universities and colleges throughout the United
Kingdom and the Republic of Ireland, and a member movement
of the International Fellowship of Evangelical Students. For
information about local and national activities write to UCCF,
38 De Montfort Street, Leicester LE1 7GP.*

Contents

Preface

Invited by the organizers of Spring Harvest Word Alive to deliver the Bible Readings that would accompany the main seminars on the Ten Commandments, I knew they had to be from Deuteronomy. The seminars would explore how the Ten Commandments can be understood and applied in today's world. They would be concentrating on God's law. There needed to be a balancing focus on God's grace, God's love, God's salvation. For some preachers, that would mean instant flight to the safety of the New Testament; grace in abundance to be found there, of course. However, that would have reinforced the sadly still common misunderstanding that the Old Testament is all about law, and that only the New Testament brings us the God of grace and love. Of all the books in the Old Testament that expose the falsehood of such a view, Deuteronomy stands out as the great declaration of God's covenant love, the celebration of God's severity and his mercy. And, of course, the Ten Commandments themselves, in one of their occurrences, are nested in Deuteronomy, surrounded by the story of redemption and the grace of forgiveness. So I wanted to make sure that those notes were clearly heard from the Old Testament itself by those who would spend the other half of their morning thinking about how to live in obedience to God's law in the world outside. For in the end, it is not just a matter of *how* we live, but of *who* we live for.

Deuteronomy challenged Israel to face up to the reality of Yahweh, the Lord, their God. They must understand who he is, his character, his actions, his sovereign purpose in their own history, and his ultimate mission of blessing the rest of the nations. They must never forget the greatness of his electing and redeeming love for them, or the horror of their constant failure to respond adequately to it. And yet his grace is such that he kept calling them back to love and loyalty, sometimes through judgment, sometimes through incredible acts of mercy. Only as they treasured this rich heritage of history and faith would they be able even to begin to obey him and walk in his ways. The same is true in principle for us as Christians. We too are called to know, love and worship, and obey the same Lord God, made known to us fully and uniquely in the person of Jesus Christ. All our practical struggle to live out the moral implications of that faith is a matter of responsive obedience to his redeeming grace. Indeed, it is all summed up by Jesus himself in the words of the greatest commandment, quoted from Deuteronomy, 'Hear, O Israel: The LORD our God, the LORD, is one. Love the LORD your God with all your heart and with all your soul and with all your strength.' The expositions that follow seek to bring out some of the depths of what motivates such love, what threatens it and what demonstrates it.

I wish to express my thanks to Word Alive for the opportunity of letting Deuteronomy speak again to another large community of people camped near the water's edge, and also to Marie Palmer for transcribing, and Anthony

Nanson for editing the written word into the present form for publication.

Chris Wright
December 1997

Knowing God

(Deuteronomy 4:1–40)

The heartbeat of Scripture

Hear now, O Israel, the decrees and laws I am about to teach you. Follow them so that you may live and may go in and take possession of the land that the LORD, the God of your fathers, is giving you. Do not add to what I command you and do not subtract from it, but keep the commands of the LORD your God that I give you.

You saw with your own eyes what the LORD did at Baal Peor. The LORD your God destroyed from among you everyone who followed the Baal of Peor, but all of you who held fast to the LORD your God are still alive today (Deuteronomy 4:1–4).

The book of Deuteronomy lies close to the very heartbeat of the Scriptures. It is to the Old Testament something like the book of Romans is to the New Testament. It deals with many of the key themes that inform the rest of the Bible. Material from Deuteronomy crops up in the prophets, the Psalms and elsewhere.

One of the objectives of this book about Deuteronomy is to look at the scriptural context in which God's law is located: a context of God's greatness, God's grace, God's redemption and God's love. An important aspect of this is the historical context in which the book is set. Deuteronomy presents itself as the speeches of Moses, at the end of his life, to the people of Israel at the point immediately before they moved into the promised land. The book opens, 'These are the words Moses spoke to all Israel in the desert east of the Jordan . . .' The Israelites were still on the far side of the Jordan, the wrong side. They were the generation after the generation of those who had come out of

Egypt in the great exodus. They were the generation who would take the land of Canaan.

A people on the move

Thus, Deuteronomy is the word of God, through Moses, to the people of God at a crucial moment in their history. They were, first of all, a people on the move. And God himself is presented here, and elsewhere in the Bible, as a God on the move. His power and presence had been felt in Egypt. His power had brought these people out of Egypt, across the sea and into the wilderness. They had enjoyed God's protection and provision as, day by day, week by week, he had travelled through the wilderness with them. Deuteronomy repeatedly says, 'The LORD your God is going ahead of you into the land.' God is on the move. God has a purpose. And so he calls his people to follow him and be a people on the move. Deuteronomy is a book for people following a purposeful God.

A people on the boundary

Secondly, Deuteronomy is a book for people on the boundary. The opening of chapter 4 says,

'Hear now, O Israel, the decrees and laws I am about to teach you. Follow them so that you may live and may go in and take possession of the land that the LORD, the God of your fathers, is giving you.' For the people of Israel, the boundary to be crossed was geographical. They were going to cross from the wilderness to a settled land. The boundary was also historical. Behind them stood the promises of God to Abraham and to the generation that had set out from Egypt. Ahead of them was an unknown future, full of danger and uncertainty. They were moving from the past to the future.

It was also a religious and cultural boundary. They had been in the wilderness, where for most of the time they had been alone with God. Now they were entering a new cultural milieu, where they would encounter enemies, idolatry, paganism – a whole new set of challenges to be faced. They were called to cross that boundary, to seize the opportunity that the previous generation had failed to seize. As Moses reminded them, their fathers and mothers had not crossed this boundary. They had reached it, then turned back because of their unbelief, their fear and their hardness of heart.

Christian mission always means crossing

boundaries. It means going with God to a place where he is not yet known and worshipped. That may mean travelling across geographical barriers, but it also means crossing barriers in ourselves and our community. The people of God, whether the Israelites in the Old Testament or ourselves today, are always facing a boundary, a place God is calling us to. Will you go and possess what God has for you, or will you do as the earlier generation of Israel did: stay put and do nothing?

A people on trial

Thirdly, Deuteronomy is the word of God to a people on trial. In 4:3–4, Moses says, 'You saw with your own eyes what the LORD did at Baal Peor. The LORD your God destroyed from among you everyone who followed the Baal of Peor, but all of you who held fast to the LORD your God are still alive today.' This refers to the most recent tragedy in the history of Israel, described in Numbers 25, when they had fallen into idolatry and immorality in Moab. Moses was challenging them about their loyalty to the God who was taking them forward into the promised land. That loyalty would be tested more than it had ever been tested before. Israel would face a new culture, new temptations, new fears, surrounded by people who did not worship the living God. Could God's people remain loyal to the God who had brought them out of Egypt, or would they simply add him to the list of Canaanite gods, making him one among many gods they would embrace?

Israel's unique position among the nations

See, I have taught you decrees and laws as the LORD my God commanded me, so that you may follow them in the land you are entering to take possession of it. Observe them carefully, for this will show your wisdom and understanding to the nations, who will hear about all these decrees and say, 'Surely this great nation is a wise and understanding people.' What other nation is so great as to have their gods near them the way the LORD our God is near us whenever we pray to him? And what other nation is so great as to have such righteous decrees and laws as this body of laws I am setting before you today? (4:5–8).

It is important, when seeking to understand the meaning and relevance of Old Testament law and the Ten Commandments, to know who the people of Israel were, the people to whom the law was given. The essence of Deuteronomy 4:5–8 is that if Israel kept God's law and lived the way he wanted them to, then this would show something to the other nations. It is significant here that into our picture of the relationship between God and Israel come the nations of the world. The obedience of the people of God is set within the arena of the world of nations which God rules over.

In the opening of the book of Genesis we are presented with a view of how the world came to be as it now is. We are shown how God is the creator of the world, the creator of humanity, and the creator of all the nations of the earth. Then we are shown how human beings rebelled and sinned against God. By Genesis 11, the episode of the Tower of Babel, we have a picture of the human race scattered, divided, and under God's wrath and curse. This is the world in which we live – the world of the nations running away from God.

The calling of Abraham

In Genesis 12, God calls Abraham. God's answer to the problems of the nations was to call a geriatric old man and woman, who had not had a child, and to tell them that they would be his answer to the problems of the world. They thought that was rather funny. And yet Abraham did believe God and obey him. God was saying, 'I have this whole world of nations, and I am calling you. Leave your home, your family, and go to the land that I will show you. I will bless you. I will make you into a great nation, and through you all the nations of the earth will be blessed.' This is the amazing manifesto of God's mission which runs through the whole of the Scriptures. It is central to Paul's theology of mission, as he explains in Romans, Galatians and elsewhere, that it was always God's purpose to bless the nations. God always had the whole world in his sights, but he would begin with one man, one family; then one people, Israel; then, through Jesus Christ, the multinational people of God throughout the world.

A light to the nations

Thus the people of Israel had a unique position in God's purposes for human history. They were a people called into existence for the blessing of the rest of the world. In other parts of the Old Testament, Israel is described as a light to go forth to the nations or a light that will attract the nations to God. In Deuteronomy 4, the people of Israel are described in terms of an example that the other nations would see. Israel's visible presence would raise questions among them. 'This is a strange people,' they would say. 'What other people have a God like this?' Many of the neighbouring polytheistic nations, including later the Romans, could not understand how one could have a God without an image of God. What sort of God would not have a statue to represent him? What sort of God would make such astounding claims to be the creator of all the world and all the nations? Moreover, as the nations looked at Israel they would see the justice and righteousness of its community. They would wonder what kind of people would have such a righteous body of laws as those that Israel had been given.

'What makes a nation great?' That was an

essay question my son put to me during his A-level history course. My answer was, 'God.' For Moses, it is the nearness of God that makes a nation great: God's presence, the acknowledgment of God, and a social system marked by righteousness and justice.

God expects that the people of God will be visible, that the nations should be able to see what we are like and should have the right to ask questions about us. It is an essential part of our mission that we recognize our unique role of representing God to other people. In order to do that, and to raise questions about God among the nations, we must live in obedience to God's law.

Before we try to apply the Ten Commandments to the nation at large, we must ask questions about ourselves, our position, and our mission as God's people. Moses told Israel they must obey God's law for a missionary reason: so that the nations would be drawn to ask questions about the God whom Israel worshipped and the way Israel lived. Jesus said something similar to his disciples. He told his motley band of fishermen and assorted riffraff:

You are the light of the world. A city on a hill

cannot be hidden. Neither do people light a lamp and put it under a bowl. Instead they put it on its stand, and it gives light to everyone in the house. In the same way, let your light shine before men, that they may see your good deeds and praise your Father in heaven (Matthew 5:14–16).

When people look at us, they should be pointed towards the God we worship.

A unique responsibility

Only be careful, and watch yourselves closely so that you do not forget the things your eyes have seen or let them slip from your heart as long as you live. Teach them to your children and to their children after them. Remember the day you stood before the LORD your God at Horeb, when he said to me, 'Assemble the people before me to hear my words so that they may learn to revere me as long as they live in the land and may teach them to their children.' You came near and stood at the foot of the mountain while it blazed with fire to the very heavens, with black clouds and deep darkness. Then the LORD spoke to you out of the fire. You heard the sound of words but saw no form; there was only a voice. He declared to you his covenant, the Ten Commandments, which he commanded you to follow and then wrote them on two stone tablets. And the LORD directed me at that time to teach you the decrees and laws you are to follow in the land that you are crossing the Jordan to possess.

You saw no form of any kind the day the LORD spoke to you at Horeb out of the fire. Therefore watch yourselves very carefully, so that you do not become corrupt and make for yourselves an idol, an image of any shape, whether formed like a man or a woman, or like any animal on earth or any bird that flies in the air, or like any creature that moves along the ground or any fish in the waters below. And when you look up to the sky and see the sun, the moon and the stars – all the heavenly array – do not be enticed into bowing down to them and worshipping things the LORD your God has apportioned to all the nations under heaven. But as for you, the LORD took you and brought you out of the iron-smelting furnace, out of Egypt, to be the people of his inheritance, as you now are (4:9–20).

The more important is your position, the greater is your responsibility for how you live. The more important your role in any situation, the more people expect something from you, and then the more vulnerable you are to failure or the temptation of compromise. When great leaders fall into sin, the impact is great, because people have looked to them for an example of how to live.

So it was for Israel. So it is for the church. God laid on Israel the task of bringing blessing to the nations. What a task Jesus laid on us, the church, when he told us to go and make disciples of all nations. What a huge responsibility. So we have to be careful how we live. The key phrase in this part of chapter 4 is 'watch yourselves': in verse 9, 'Only be careful, and watch yourselves closely . . .'; again in verse 15, 'Therefore watch yourselves very carefully . . .'; and in verse 23, 'Be careful . . .' The same Hebrew word is used in all three instances.

The danger of idolatry

The key warning here is against idolatry. That is the great enemy of God's people, and the great threat to their witness to the nations. The nations already follow their own gods. So if we, the people chosen to bring the knowledge of the living God to the nations, go after their gods, there will be no difference between us and them, and no witness, no message, no mission.

How do you keep from idolatry? First, says Moses, 'be careful . . . that you *do not forget* . . .' (verse 9). There is great emphasis in Deuteronomy on remembering what God has done. The Israelites were told not to forget all that they had experienced in being brought out of Egypt. Nor to forget the Ten Commandments. They were to teach these to their children and to each succeeding generation. Among the people of God there should be constant teaching and learning of what God has done and the great truths he has taught us.

The reason why it is so important to teach the word of God is our missionary calling to represent God to the nations. That is our responsibility. Therefore, to fulfil that task, we must keep ourselves from idolatry – and to do that, we need to be well taught.

Things that dazzle

Secondly, says Moses, '*do not be enticed*' (4:19).

When we look up at the sky and see the sun, moon and stars, the great realities of creation, we must not be enticed into worshipping them. Moses recognizes here that there is something deeply attractive about idolatry. When we think of idolatry, we tend to think of strange practices in foreign countries, strange and horrible things we would never do ourselves. But our idolatry concerns the things that *do* attract us, that dazzle our sensibilities.

In 4:16–19, the list of possible sources of idolatry inverts the order of creation. In Genesis 1 the creation begins with light, the sun and the heavens, then the earth, the seas, the fish, then the land, the animals, and finally human beings. Perhaps it is significant that in a warning against idolatry that order is reversed, as if to say that if you do not put the living God first, then everything else is turned upside down. We end up with a life and a society that are out of order, chaotic and absurd, that call evil good, and good evil.

The Israelites were warned to be careful what they laid their eyes on and let themselves be dazzled by. They were reminded that when God spoke to them, it was not what they saw with their eyes that mattered, but what they heard with their ears. When they experienced the reality of God at Mount Sinai (also known as Horeb), they saw no form, no dazzling statues. God came amidst an elemental performance of thunder, light and fire; but in the end it was not what they saw that counted; it was the voice that they heard. God is the living God who speaks, who has a word to give us, a word of promise, command and prohibition.

Two possible futures

The LORD was angry with me because of you, and he solemnly swore that I would not cross the Jordan and enter the good land the LORD your God is giving you as your inheritance. I will die in this land; I will not cross the Jordan; but you are about to cross over and take possession of that good land. Be careful not to forget the covenant of the LORD your God that he made with you; do not make for yourselves an idol in the form of anything the LORD your God has forbidden. For the LORD your God is a consuming fire, a jealous God.

After you have had children and grand-children and have lived in the land a long time – if you then become corrupt and make any kind of idol, doing evil in the eyes of the LORD your God and provoking him to anger, I call heaven and earth as witnesses against you this day that you will quickly perish from the land that you are crossing the Jordan to possess. You will not live there long but will certainly be destroyed. The LORD will scatter you among the peoples, and only a few of you will survive among the nations to which the LORD will drive you. There you will worship man-made gods of wood and stone, which cannot see or hear or eat or smell. But if from there you seek the LORD your God, you will find him if you look for him with all your heart and with all your soul. When you are in distress and all these things have happened to you, then in later days you will return to the LORD your God and obey him. For the LORD your God is a merciful God; he will not abandon or destroy you or forget the covenant with your forefathers, which he confirmed to them by oath (4:21–31).

Why does it matter whether or not we, the people of God, take seriously our unique responsibility? Because we have to face this living God. In 4:23–31, Moses anticipates two possible futures for Israel, in both of which they must face God.

The first is the reversal of the promise to Abraham. Instead of being many, Israel would become few. As we know from the rest of the Old Testament, that was in fact the route down which Israel went. They went that way and crashed into the God who is jealous, a consuming fire, the God whose love cannot abide any competitors (verse 24). But in verses 29–31, we see the alternative future, of repentance, return and restoration. When you go down that road you meet the God who is merciful, who will not abandon, destroy or forget you (verse 31).

We are presented with this duality within God. He is either a consuming fire, jealous for his name, who will not tolerate idolatry among his people, or he is a God of mercy and compassion, slow to anger and abounding in love, who will never forget his people. This does not mean that God is changeable. God is consistent in his encounter with a tragically inconsistent people.

One reason why the book of Deuteronomy is so significant is that it anticipates the reality of Israel's course through history – through their exile and their restoration from exile – to Christ.

The same pattern is repeated time and again in the history of God's people, including the church and our own individual lives.

A unique experience

Ask now about the former days, long before your time, from the day God created man on the earth; ask from one end of the heavens to the other. Has anything so great as this ever happened, or has anything like it ever been heard of? Has any other people heard the voice of God speaking out of fire, as you have, and lived? Has any god ever tried to take for himself one nation out of another nation, by testings, by miraculous signs and wonders, by war, by a mighty hand and an outstretched arm, or by great and awesome deeds, like all the things the LORD your God did for you in Egypt before your very eyes? (4:32–34).

Still the questions come back to us. Why should we accept such a position and responsibility? Why take seriously this warning against idolatry? In the climactic part of chapter 4 comes Moses' answer (verses 32–34): it is because no other people has experienced what we have experienced of God. The questions Moses poses are rhetorical. The answer to all of them is 'no'. No other nation had experienced what God had done for Israel. God had done nothing like this in any other context in any other time. Israel's experience of God, therefore, was unique.

Revelation

First, Israel's experience of God's revelation was unparalleled. At Mount Sinai, God made known to Israel, through Moses, his own character, his covenant, his law and all that he wanted for his people. No other people had been given such a revelation. A similar affirmation is made in Psalm 147: '[God] has revealed his word to Jacob, his laws and decrees to Israel. He has done this for no other nation; they do not know his laws' (147:19–20). Neither Moses nor the psalmist means that no other people except Israel had any idea about morality. The whole of the Scriptures makes it clear that *all* human beings made in the image of God understand something about who God is and about the fundamental moral requirements of human life. But there is something unique about what God revealed to Israel. That nation knew God in a way that no other people then did.

Redemption

Secondly, Israel's experience of redemption was unique. The exodus, God's great act of deliverance, was as important historically and theologically for Israel as the cross and resurrection of Jesus are for Christians now. It was the monumental proof of God's love, his faithfulness to his word, and his redemptive power and grace. It was the basis of everything that God did for his people thereafter.

The Israelites were reminded of this at Mount Sinai. In Exodus 19, God speaks to them from the mountain:

'You yourselves have seen what I did to Egypt, and how I carried you on eagles' wings and brought you to myself. Now if you obey me fully and keep my covenant, then out of all nations you will be my treasured possession. Although the whole earth is mine, you will be for me a kingdom of priests and a holy nation.' These are the words you are to speak to the Israelites (19:4–6).

Israel had experienced God's salvation in a way no other nation had. Therefore they had a missionary responsibility to be the priesthood of God among the nations. To them was entrusted the knowledge of God for the other nations. The same identity and mission is laid upon Christians. In 1 Peter 2, the apostle Peter speaks to a mixed gathering of Christians, consisting not just of Jewish believers but of people from many regions. He quotes from Exodus and other parts of the Old Testament, and says to these people and to us, '. . . you are a chosen people, a royal priesthood, a holy nation, a people belonging to God . . .' (1 Peter 2:9). That is our identity. Our purpose is to 'declare the praises of him who called you out of darkness into his wonderful light'. That is the language of exodus. Peter is reminding us that we have experienced our own exodus. We may not have come out of Egypt, but we have come out of darkness, out of sin, out of the kingdom of Satan. God has brought us into the kingdom of his marvellous light. Therefore we have the responsibility of making this known. That is why, in 1 Peter 2:12, Peter says, 'Live such good lives among the pagans that, though they accuse you of doing wrong, they may see your good deeds and glorify God on the day he visits us.'

These words are for us. We should accept the mission of being God's people in the world, because our experience of God is unique. It is not merely that each of us has a unique personal experience of the living God who, through Jesus Christ, has revealed himself to us and saved us – though that is true. But the Christian experience of all of us is based upon the life and death and resurrection of the Lord Jesus Christ and the fact that in his name, and in no other, there is forgiveness and salvation. That is a unique reality, a unique message entrusted to us. It is ours by God's grace, not to keep to ourselves but to share with the nations.

A unique God

You were shown these things so that you might know that the LORD is God; besides him there is no other. From heaven he made you hear his voice to discipline you. On earth he showed you his great fire, and you heard his words from out of the fire. Because he loved your forefathers and chose their descendants after them, he brought you out of Egypt by his Presence and his great strength,

to drive out before you nations greater and
stronger than you and to bring you into their
land to give it to you for your inheritance, as
it is today.

Acknowledge and take to heart this day that
the LORD is God in heaven above and on the
earth below. There is no other. Keep his
decrees and commands, which I am giving
you today, so that it may go well with you
and your children after you and that you may
live long in the land the LORD your God
gives you for all time (4:35–40).

All the way through this chapter 4 of Deuteronomy, we can imagine the Israelites or
ourselves asking 'why?' Now the question
comes again: why have we had this experience?
The answer is in verse 35: 'You were shown
these things so that you might know that the
LORD is God; besides him there is no other.'
And in verse 39: 'Acknowledge and take to
heart this day that the LORD is God in heaven
above and on the earth below. There is no
other.' Thus the purpose of what the Israelites
had been through becomes clear. They had
experienced all that they had so that they
would know who the living God is. Other

nations did not yet know, but they did. Yahweh, the Lord, is God, and there is no other.

The text does not say that they were shown these things so they might believe in God, or so they might know that there is only one God, or so they might be extra-specially religious. The point is not the difference between atheism and belief, or between monotheism and polytheism. The question is: if everybody believes in a God of some sort, who really is God? The text says that the people of Israel had been given this unique experience of revelation and redemption so that they would know that Yahweh, the Lord, is God. It is about the *character* of God. Yahweh is the God of mercy, compassion, justice and liberation, the God who brought them out of Egypt and protected them in the wilderness, the God of Abraham, Isaac and Jacob – this is God.

It is amazing how often commentators want to evade the monotheistic claim of these verses. They say that the text does not actually mean there was no other God at all: no other God *for Israel*, perhaps, but their faith was not true monotheism. Yet verse 39 says, '. . . the LORD [Yahweh] is God in heaven above and on the earth below. There is no other.' There is nowhere else for any other God to be. These verses strongly affirm the uniqueness of Israel's God.

Throughout her history, Israel lost touch with this truth and worshipped other gods. And so have Christians. But this affirmation in Deuteronomy is essentially the same as, and forms the foundation of, the New Testament claim that Jesus is Lord and there is no other. When the early Christians came to recognize who Jesus was, they affirmed his uniqueness in the terms they already knew – the uniqueness of Yahweh. Jesus completed the mission of Israel. He incarnated the unique God of Israel, and he was therefore unique himself.

We have come almost full circle. In this chapter of Deuteronomy, the people of God are told that they know the unique God of the universe. They know that because they have experienced him. He has invaded their under-standing. He spoke to them at Mount Sinai. He brought them out of Egypt. Why? Because he has called them to be a blessing and a witness to the nations, a people to represent the living God to other peoples. This is Israel's mission and identity. The conclusion comes in verse 40: 'Keep his decrees and commands, which I am giving you today, so that it may go well with you . . .' Keep the Ten Commandments; obey them and live by them. But understand the reason why: because you know the God who gave them, you know the God who saved you, you know the God who calls you to be his witness among the nations of the world, so that the nations will come to recognize that the Lord is God and there is no other.

Loving God

(Deuteronomy 6:1–25)

These are the commands, decrees and laws the LORD your God directed me to teach you to observe in the land that you are crossing the Jordan to possess, so that you, your children and their children after them may fear the LORD your God as long as you live by keeping all his decrees and commands that I give you, and so that you may enjoy long life. Hear, O Israel, and be careful to obey so that it may go well with you and that you may increase greatly in a land flowing with milk and honey, just as the LORD, the God of your fathers, promised you (6:1–3).

On one occasion in the gospels, one of the teachers of the law came and asked Jesus which was the greatest commandment in the law. It was not a new question, nor in one sense was Jesus' answer new. The rabbis were much given to debating which of the commandments was the most important – and which the least. They had come to the conclusion that the least of the commandments was one in Deuteronomy which says that if you find a mother bird on its nest with eggs or chicks, you may take the eggs or chicks but not the mother bird. We may regard that as a good ecological principle. The rabbis, though they regarded it as the least important commandment in the law, noted that it is motivated by the same theological promise as the fifth of the Ten Commandments: '. . . so that you may live long in the land the LORD your God is giving you' (Exodus 20:12). They concluded that if the least of the laws is based on that premise, then how much more the rest of the law.

In Jesus' response to the question about the greatest commandment, he quoted from Deuteronomy 6 and Leviticus 19. '"Love the Lord your God with all your heart and with all your soul and with all your mind." This is the first and greatest commandment. And the second is like it:

"Love your neighbour as yourself."' What was unusual in Jesus' reply was not his selection of these two commandments, but that he then went on to say, 'All the Law and the Prophets hang on these two commandments' (Matthew 22:37–40). These are not simply the first two of a long list of commandments; rather, they constitute the fundamental principle beneath the whole of the Old Testament law. Let us look from this perspective at Deuteronomy 6 and the command to 'Love the LORD your God'.

Love commanded

> Hear, O Israel: The LORD our God, the LORD is one. Love the LORD your God with all your heart and with all your soul and with all your strength. These commandments that I give you today are to be upon your hearts. Impress them on your children. Talk about them when you sit at home and when you walk along the road, when you lie down and when you get up. Tie them as symbols on your hands and bind them on your foreheads. Write them on the door-frames of your houses and on your gates (6:4–9).

Deuteronomy 6:4–5 is the central creed of the Jewish faith. It is sometimes called the *Shema'*, from the opening words, 'Shema' Israel' ('Hear, O Israel'). Its significance for Jewish people is similar to that for Christians of the statement 'Jesus is Lord', or for Muslims of 'There is no God but Allah, and Muhammad is his prophet'. Although it is a defining credal statement for the Jews, it is also affirmed by Christians, as it was by Jesus.

The two verses are, respectively, a proposition and a command. Verse 4 tells us that the Lord, Yahweh, is one. Verse 5 commands us to love him. A statement of truth, followed by a personal response. This is significant for biblical faith. You may hear the notion that religious faith is different from everyday truth: religious truth is personal and relational, rather than propositional. In fact, biblical truth has the qualities of both personal, relational experience and the timeless statements of propositional truth. Verse 4 could not be more propositional. It makes a dogmatic, explicit statement: 'The LORD our God, the LORD is one.' But it is immediately followed by a personal, relational command: 'Love the LORD your God with all your heart and with all your soul and with all your strength.'

One God, Yahweh

The footnotes in your Bible will tell you that there are several ways in which the statement in Deuteronomy 6:4 can be translated. In the Hebrew it consists of just four words: 'Yahweh, our God, Yahweh, one' ('our God' being just one word in Hebrew). It is a matter of debate exactly where you put the verb 'is'. I think the New International Version's phrasing has got it right. It affirms the oneness of Yahweh our God, consistent with the declaration in Deuteronomy 4:35 and 39 that Yahweh alone is God in heaven above and on earth beneath and there is no other. According to some scholars it means the same as those verses: Yahweh alone is God. However, the words in Hebrew for 'one' and 'alone' are not the same, so if in 6:4 the writer had wanted to say, 'The LORD is God, the LORD alone', he could have said it in a slightly different way. So we should take the verse to mean that Yahweh is one single God, not a brand name for a set of gods that share this name.

Such collective naming of gods was characteristic of other religions of the time. Baal, for example, was a very general name. Baal, son of El, was one of the Canaanite pantheon of gods, but the term 'Baal' could be applied to various divine powers. The Canaanites could never have said, 'Baal is one', or even comprehended the idea of such a statement. Our text is asserting, quite distinctively from the surrounding polytheistic religions, that Yahweh is God, Yahweh is our God, and Yahweh is one God. He is a singular God, with his own integrity, character, will and purpose; one God whom we are to worship.

Theological terms like 'deity', 'covenant' and 'monotheism' can sound very abstract. Here they are given life and colour through the naming of the God with whom they are associated. Yahweh is *our* God, so the covenant is defined by Yahweh. Yahweh is *one* God, so monotheism is defined by Yahweh.

Old Testament Israelites were called upon to acknowledge this truth of the one God, to repeat it, to recite it, to believe it, and to look forward to the day when all nations would acknowledge it. We have already seen how important it is to recognize Deuteronomy's expectation that God would bless all the nations through the people of Israel. Zechariah 14 is another chapter that looks forward to the future. The vision presented there declares, '[In that day] the LORD will be king over the whole earth. On that day there will be one LORD, and his name the only name' (Zechariah 14:9). The Israelites were well aware that this spoke of something that had yet to become true among the nations of the world. But there would come a day when Yahweh would be the king of all the world and his name would be the one name acknowledged by the world. Thus the simple propositional statement 'The LORD our God is one God' can become a prophetic vision. When we see this text in the light of Jesus and the church's mission, this truth is affirmed, but with Jesus right at the heart of it. The uniqueness of Jesus is rooted in the uniqueness of Yahweh, the God of Israel.

One Lord, Jesus

When thinking about what distinguishes Christianity from other religions, we should not start comparing one religion against another. To do that implies that Jesus came along to found a new religion in the same way that Muhammad founded Islam and Buddha founded Buddhism. Jesus did not come with the intention of starting a new religion. He came as the one who brought fulfilment and completion to all that God had done through the history of his people and through the revelation of the Scriptures. When the early disciples recognized that in Jesus of Nazareth the Lord God himself had walked among them, they recognized the fulfilment of all that God had promised.

In 1 Corinthians 8, Paul discusses one of the problems that arose out of the struggles of early Christian mission. Mission involves answering problems related to the context in which people are living. In Corinth there was a problem over idols. The meat market and the temples existed in happy symbiosis, such that the meat that was sacrificed to the gods was then eaten by humans. Responding to the Corinthian Christians' worries about that situation, Paul wrote,

So then, about eating food sacrificed to idols: We know that an idol is nothing at all in the world and that there is no God but one. For even if there are so-called gods, whether in heaven or on earth (as indeed there are many 'gods' and many 'lords'), yet for us there is but one God, the Father, from whom all things came and for whom we live; and there is but one Lord, Jesus Christ, through whom all things came and through whom we live (1 Corinthians 8:4–6).

Throughout that passage we see Paul's Jewish monotheistic faith coming through. Paul's concern was to ensure that the church should be scriptural (in terms of the writings that we now call the Old Testament, and in contrast to our contemporary problem of whether we can believe that the Old Testament is Christian). Paul takes his scriptural (Old Testament) understanding of one God, one Lord, and builds into it the centre of the revelation of God as the Lord Jesus Christ, the creator and the saviour. A theologian would call this a christological expansion of the *Shema'*.

A strong word

'Love the LORD your God with all your heart and with all your soul and with all your strength.' The word 'love' occurs about eight times in Deuteronomy in this connection. For example:

And now, O Israel, what does the LORD your God ask of you but to fear the LORD your

God, to walk in all his ways, to love him, to serve the LORD your God with all your heart and with all your soul, and to observe the LORD's commands . . . (10:12–13).

Love the LORD your God and keep his requirements, his decrees, his laws and his commands always (11:1).

So if you faithfully obey the commands I am giving you today – to love the LORD your God and to serve him with all your heart and with all your soul . . . (11:13).

Towards the end of the book, we are told,

The LORD your God will circumcise your hearts and the hearts of your descendants, so that you may love him with all your heart and with all your soul, and live (30:6).

And a few verses later on, love is made a matter of life and death:

See, I set before you today life and prosperity, death and destruction. For I command you today to love the LORD your God, to walk in his ways . . . (30:15–16).

So 'love' is a strong word here. That love was to be shown through loyalty and obedience.

The same motif recurs in the New Testament. In the gospel of John, Jesus says, 'If you love me, you will obey what I command' (John 14:15). Those words might easily have come from Deuteronomy. As John says in 1 John, you cannot say that you love God if you go and disobey him by hating your brother (1 John 4:20).

Heart and soul

Deuteronomy 6:5 amplifies the command to love God 'with all your heart and with all your soul and with all your strength'. God is one whole single God, so you must love him with the whole single you. All that you are must be given to the love of God. 'Heart' and 'soul' are referred to repeatedly in Deuteronomy, but what exactly did those terms mean to the Israelites?

For us, the heart often symbolizes the emotional dimension of love, for example on Valentine cards or in expressions like 'I love you with all my heart'. The Israelites recognized that dimension, but they perceived the heart more as the seat of the mind than of the emotions. They had not the anatomical knowledge to make clear distinctions between the functions of the brain, the heart and other parts of the body. If he felt really emotional, an Israelite man might have told his wife, 'I love you with all my bowels'! The heart was the organ of the will. It was where you made decisions and choices. That is why there is so much in the book of Proverbs about the heart: 'Above all else, guard your heart' (Proverbs 4:23).

As for the soul, that seems to us a vague spiritual thing; we are not quite sure what it is or where it is inside us. Correctly, it is the inner person, you as you know yourself to be. We are to love God with our mind and heart and that inner self.

Mind and strength

In the gospels, where this verse is translated into Greek, the word 'mind' has been included. This is probably to explain for Greek-speaking readers what 'the heart' really means: 'Love the Lord your God with all your heart and soul and all your mind and strength.'

It is important to recognize that God commands us to love him with our minds and not just our emotions. One of the most unfortunate dichotomies in much Christian thinking and practice is that between the spiritual and the intellectual. People get the idea that there is a cleavage between our mind and our feelings. This is tragic, because we are commanded by the Bible to love God with our minds. I tell my students, 'unless you *think* about the Scriptures and *think* about the world and your mission, you will not be much use for the Lord. Love the Lord, but love him with your mind as well as your heart, and with everything else that you are.'

The third expression in Deuteronomy 6:5, 'and with all your strength', occurs only once elsewhere in the whole Old Testament as this addendum to the combination of heart and soul (see 2 Kings 23:25). Translated literally, it means 'with your very muchness'. The word does not usually occur as a noun but as an emphasis of an action – to do something *very much*. Here the implication is that you are to love God with all your heart and with all your soul and with total excess overflowing. There are no limits on loving God. You can never say you have loved him enough.

In private and in public

How often have you heard people say that the difference between the Old Testament and the New Testament is that in the former the law was written on stone, whereas in the latter it is to be written in our hearts?

Here in Deuteronomy, God is clearly saying that these laws are to be in your heart and your mind. It is not only an external code of law, but a part of ordinary everyday life, from breakfast to bedtime, when you are out of the house and when you come home. This does not mean that you should do nothing else in life but recite the law and read the Scriptures. However, 6:8–9 makes it clear that God's law is to impinge on the choices you make in every aspect of your life: choices related to the home and the road, your hands and your head, the things you do and the things you think. The word 'gate' in verse 9 refers not to a garden gate but to the gates of the city, the place of public concourse. The gate was the marketplace, the law courts, the whole public arena. The law of God is to apply in your private life (hands), your family life (door posts) and your public life (gates).

It is sad how these things get separated. When

a politician gets caught with his pants down, some people will say that his private life is irrelevant and has no bearing on his public life. I accept that people need privacy and protection, but it is nonsense to say that what you are in private has no bearing on what you are in public. If people feel free in private to ignore, say, God's seventh commandment, about adultery, or the tenth commandment, about covetousness, then what reason have we for trusting they might be inclined to obey the eighth commandment, about theft, or the ninth commandment, about telling the truth?

So, then, love is commanded. One Lord, one love, one life.

Love endangered

When the LORD your God brings you into the land he swore to your fathers, to Abraham, Isaac and Jacob, to give you – a land with large, flourishing cities you did not build, houses filled with all kinds of good things you did not provide, wells you did not dig, and vineyards and olive groves you did not plant – then when you eat and are satisfied, be careful that you do not forget the LORD, who brought you out of Egypt, out of the land of slavery.

Fear the LORD your God, serve him only and take your oaths in his name. Do not follow other gods, the gods of the peoples around you; for the LORD your God, who is among you, is a jealous God and his anger will burn against you, and he will destroy you from the face of the land. Do not test the LORD your God as you did at Massah. Be sure to keep the commands of the LORD your God and the stipulations and decrees he has given you. Do what is right and good in the LORD's sight, so that it may go well with you and you may go in and take over the good land that the LORD promised on oath to your forefathers, thrusting out all your enemies before you, as the LORD said (6:10–19).

A colleague of mine, Walter Riggans, when preaching at College once said, 'You know, Romans tells us that nothing can separate us from the love of God. But there are a million things that can separate God from our love.' Nothing will ever stop God loving us, but there is plenty that will stop us from loving God. Moses was aware of that. In 6:10–19 he describes three dangers that can threaten our love for God. Each is introduced with the words 'do not . . .'. In verse 12, '. . . do not forget the LORD, who brought you out of Egypt, out of the land of slavery'; in verse 14, 'Do not follow other gods . . .'; and in verse 16, 'Do not test the LORD your God . . .'

Affluence

Deuteronomy 6:10–12 warns us of the danger that affluence may lead us to forget God. This theme is expanded in chapter 8:

When you have eaten and are satisfied, praise the LORD your God for the good land he has given you. Be careful that you do not forget the LORD your God, failing to observe his commands, his laws and his decrees that I am giving you this day. Otherwise, when you eat and are satisfied, when you build fine houses and settle down, and when your herds and flocks grow large and your silver and gold increase and all you have is multiplied, then your heart will become proud and you will forget the LORD your God, who brought you out of Egypt . . . You may say to yourself, 'My power and the strength of my hands have produced this wealth for me.' But remember the LORD your God, for it is he who gives you the ability to produce wealth, and so confirms his covenant, which he swore to your forefathers, as it is today (8:10–18).

The temptation is that, when things are going well, we want to take the credit. The boastfulness of the human heart is universal. We like to think that whatever we do well is to our credit. In verses 12–13 we have a perceptive description of the tycoon's boast: '*My* hand, *my* energy, *my* effort, *my* work, *my* gifts, *my* entrepreneurial activities – have produced this wealth for *me*.' It is both boastful and selfish, and something of which we must beware.

This is one of the greatest flaws in the prosperity gospel. That particular theology teaches that prosperity is a mark of God's blessing. This is partially true in the Scriptures, but the Bible recognizes that people can be very prosperous by God's blessing and yet forget God and disobey him.

Cultural pressures

The second danger is to abandon God because of social pressures. 'Do not follow other gods, the gods of the peoples around you . . .' (6:14). When the Israelites entered Canaan, they were surrounded by a culture that was successful by the standards of that time. Canaanite civilization might have been morally degenerate but its progress in agriculture, urbanization and literacy was excellent. It was a prosperous international civilization. And Baal was its god. Baal was the god of money, of the land, of business, of fertility, of sex; he was the god of everything that mattered. So it might have seemed a good idea, in addition to worshipping Yahweh, to get on the right side of Baal and certain other gods.

The temptation is to slide into worshipping the gods of the society amidst which you live. That is what Israel did, for centuries. And Christians too, in every generation, have been tempted to abandon our God, his demands and his truth, for the gods of the people around us.

David Jackman has spoken of a 'self-obsessed kind of Christianity which mirrors the self-obsession of our society'. The content of some Christian books, films and songs differs little from the theme of self-fulfilment which is celebrated in our secular magazines and entertainment. You can have a better sex life if you go down this road. You can have a better healing ministry if you go down that road. Things are marketed in such powerful ways that you are led into pursuing the idolatries of our age. In the letter to the Romans, Paul warns Christians, 'Do not conform any longer to the pattern of this world, but be transformed by the renewing of your mind' (Romans 12:2). Do not let the world squeeze you into its mould (see J. B. Phillips' translation), but instead conform to what it means to love the living God.

Hardship

Thirdly, 'Do not test the LORD your God as you did at Massah' (6:16). Massah was the first place the Israelites reached after they had departed from Egypt (Exodus 17). They had walked a long way and were very thirsty. They came to a place where there was water but it was undrinkable. There was a tumult of complaining. They questioned whether God was really with them and really meant the things he had said. This is what is meant here by testing God –

the kind of testing that springs from unbelief and rebellion. It should not be confused with testing God in the sense, sometimes used, of fully trusting him at a time when you are to take a step of faith with him.

The opening verses of Deuteronomy 8 pertain to the kind of temptation that Jesus faced in the wilderness. There, after his baptism, he was tested. He was hungry from fasting. He was struggling physically and mentally, and he was struggling spiritually with his future. Let us imagine Jesus reflecting on these words in Deuteronomy 8:2:

> Remember how the LORD your God led you all the way in the desert these forty years, to humble you and to test you in order to know what was in your heart, whether or not you would keep his commands. He humbled you, causing you to hunger and then feeding you with manna, which neither you nor your fathers had known . . .

Imagine Jesus tempted in his hunger, the devil suggesting that if he really were the Son of God he could turn some stones into bread for himself. Jesus remembered the context of the scripture the devil was using against him, that God fed the Israelites in order 'to teach you that man does not live on bread alone but on every word that comes from the mouth of the LORD ... Know ... in your heart that as a man disciplines his son, so the LORD your God disciplines you' (8:3, 5). Jesus was able to meet the temptation brought by hardship and need, through reflecting more deeply on the Scriptures and the importance of loving God (Matthew 4:4, 7, 10).

Real hardship, real need, hunger, thirst, poverty and suffering are very real challenges to our love for God. We need to recognize the truth of our feelings. I remember the first time in my Christian life that I was prepared to admit that I was angry with God. It is one thing to be angry with him; it is another to recognize that you are. I had been brought up always to trust God and to believe he was doing things for the best. But in the year before I went to work in India, I came to the point of saying, 'God, I don't know what you're doing in this situation; me and my family we're struggling here and we can't see the future, and I haven't got a job, and I don't know what lies ahead, and, God, it shouldn't be like this.' That particular situation was certainly not as severe as many other needs in the world, but it was tough enough for me to be tempted to wallow in self-pity and anger and frustration, and to lose my love for God. You yourself may be going through a crisis or some ongoing torment of need or suffering, which is causing you to test God, to doubt whether he really means what he says, whether he really loves you at all, or whether it is worth your continuing to love God. The challenge of this text comes back to us. Whether we are facing abundance or need, we are commanded to love the Lord our God with all our heart, with all our soul, with all our strength. How much does your love for God match up to the demands of Deuteronomy 6:5, the details of 6:6–9, and the dangers of 6:10–19?

Van Morrison has a wonderful song that goes, 'Have I told you lately that I love you? Have I told you there's no one above you?' It is a love song, but we can address it to God. Have you told God lately that you love him? That there is no-one above him? And that he is everything to you, no matter what life brings?

Love motivated

In the future, when your son asks you, 'What is the meaning of the stipulations, decrees and laws the LORD our God has commanded you?' tell him: 'We were slaves of Pharaoh in Egypt, but the LORD brought us out of Egypt with a mighty hand. Before our eyes the LORD sent miraculous signs and wonders – great and terrible – upon Egypt and Pharaoh and his whole household. But he brought us out from there to bring us in and give us the land that he promised on oath to our forefathers. The LORD commanded us to obey all these decrees and to fear the LORD our God, so that we might always prosper and be kept alive, as is the case today. And if we are careful to obey all this law before the LORD our God, as he has commanded us, that will be our righteousness' (6:20–25).

In these verses we face again the question 'why?' What reason is there to obey the law of God and thus prove that we love him? In this text that question is put in the mouth of a child. We must assume that the son is living in a family that is obedient to God's law. The question would not arise otherwise. When the son asks about the meaning of the law, what he wants to know is its purpose. Much of Deuteronomy is concerned with answering that question; it is law preached to people, with the reasoning given as to why they should keep it. If Christian scholars down the ages had paid more attention to Deuteronomy 6:20–25, they might have avoided some of the highways and byways they have followed trying to answer the question, 'What is the point of the Old Testament law?'

In answering his son's question, the father could simply have answered, 'You keep the law because the Lord our God has commanded it.' All parents know the temptation, when their children ask 'why?', to say, 'Stop saying "why?" and just do it because I tell you.'

At one level that would have been a perfectly acceptable reply. Why keep God's law? Because it *is* God's law! But the child might have responded like Pharaoh, who, when Moses told him Yahweh's command to 'let my people go', asked who this Yahweh was. He did not recognize Yahweh, so he would not keep his commands. If the only reason to keep God's law was that it was God's law, many people would simply ignore it. And so the father answers his son with the story of the exodus. If the son has in mind any shadow of an idea that keeping the law is like being a slave to the law, the father is addressing that. For the Israelites really had been slaves in Egypt and God had brought them out of that land in a great act of liberation. That is the reason for keeping his law.

Many Christians make the mistake of differentiating between the Old and New Testaments by saying that in the Old Testament salvation is by law and in the New Testament salvation is by grace. This is comparable to one distortion of the Scriptures which the apostle Paul attacked. People had come to believe that, to make sure they were within the covenant people, obedience to the law was essential; this was what defined the saved people of God. That could lead into various forms of pride or legalism. Paul insisted that it was never meant to be like that. The gospel always was a matter of God's grace and our response. When people raised questions about Moses (as, for example, in Galatians), Paul took them right back to Abraham. He reminded them that Abraham believed God's promises and so was counted righteous (Galatians 3:6–8). God's grace comes before the law and before our obedience.

Even the structure of the book of Exodus reinforces this. There are eighteen chapters about salvation before there is a single chapter of law. All obedience is responsive to what God has already done for us. We keep the law because God has redeemed us from slavery and brought us into righteousness. When Deuteronomy 6:25 says 'that will be our righteousness', it does not mean that we will then have earned righteousness. That would be inconsistent with the whole message of the book. It is saying that God has already saved us, and so the *right thing to do* is to love God and obey him. That is *our* righteous response to *his* righteous act of salvation.

In 4:5–8 we saw a forward-looking missionary motivation for obedience to God's law – we obey in order to show the nations the truth about God. Here we have a motivation for obedience that looks back to the story of salvation and is founded on God's redemptive grace. We love because he first loved us. We forgive each other as God in Christ has forgiven us. The dynamic is the same in both Old and New Testaments. It is what God has done for us that leads us in response to obey him. Obedience is love motivated by redemption – as much in the Old as the New Testament.

Confronting God

(Deuteronomy 9:1–20)

In many chapters of Deuteronomy, Moses engages in an imaginary dialogue with what the Israelites might have been saying to themselves. That is what good preachers often do. A good example is Deuteronomy 7:6–7 where Moses challenges any thought the Israelites might have had that God loved them because they were somehow superior to other nations. 'The LORD did not set his affection on you and choose you because you were more numerous than other peoples, for you were the fewest of all peoples.' God was not impressed by any claim that Israel was a great and mighty people. They were a tiny nation surrounded by great empires, but God loved them because he had a purpose for them, to bless the nations.

Deuteronomy 8:17 conveys something similar: 'You may say to yourself, "My power and the strength of my hands have produced this wealth for me."' In addition to the racial arrogance suggested in the previous chapter, Moses considers here a kind of economic arrogance and quickly deflates it in 8:18. Then in 9:4 he targets the assertion of self-righteousness: 'After the LORD your God has driven [those nations] out before you, do not say to yourself "The LORD has brought me here to take possession of this land because of my righteousness."'

There is an instinctive human temptation to give credit to ourselves – in terms of racism or economic materialism or moral superiority – especially in the wake of military victory. In each case, God says it is wrong to think that way.

The viewpoint presented now by chapter 9 is in terms of God's judgment, and yet if we read carefully we can see the grace of God flooding through. The first part of the chapter provides a description of God's judgment of the wicked, and the moral implications to be drawn from that. The second part deals with God's judgment of his own people, and the consequences of that.

Judgment of the wicked

Hear, O Israel. You are now about to cross the Jordan to go in and dispossess nations greater and stronger than you, with large cities that have walls up to the sky. The people are tall and strong – Anakites! You know about them and have heard it said: 'Who can stand up against the Anakites?' But be assured today that the LORD your God is the one who goes across ahead of you like a devouring fire. He will destroy them; he will subdue them before you. And you will drive them out and annihilate them quickly, as the LORD has promised you.

After the LORD your God has driven them out before you, do not say to yourself, 'The LORD has brought me here to take possession of this land because of my righteousness.' No, it is on account of the wickedness of these nations that the LORD is going to drive them out before you. It is not because of your righteousness or your integrity that you are going in to take possession of their land; but on account of the wickedness of these nations, the LORD your God will drive them out before you, to accomplish what he swore to your fathers, to Abraham, Isaac and Jacob. Understand, then, that it is not because of your righteousness that the LORD your God is giving you this good land to possess, for you are a stiff-necked people (9:1–6).

Thus chapter 9 begins with the reassurance of God's presence and power, and the promise that he would go ahead of the Israelites and win victory over their enemies. The previous generation would not believe that and had failed. Moses is now encouraging the next generation to go forward. Though Israel would have to do the physical fighting, the initiative and the power would come from God. This passage raises several issues.

Credit for the victory

First, when the battles were over and the dust had settled, what then? In the euphoria of the

Israelites' victory would come the temptation to congratulate themselves, to say to themselves that they had achieved all these victories because they were so great and righteous, because they were the ones that God favoured.

Through Moses, God reminds them that they cannot take any credit for being the people of God. That was simply due to the fact that God loved them and had chosen them. As they could take no credit for their election, so could they take no credit for their victories. We are not Christians because we deserve to be, nor do we go on being Christians because we deserve to be. In both our calling and the progression of our Christian lives, we depend on God's grace and power and not on our own righteousness.

We see in 9:4–6 how Moses answers the people's questions. The New International Version uses quotation marks partway through verse 4 for the people's claim '"The LORD has brought me here to take possession of this land because of my righteousness"' – but not for the following sentence, which reads as Moses' reply: 'it is on account of the wickedness of these nations that the LORD is going to drive them out before you'. This may be misleading. The Israelites were probably inclined to claim that

God had won them the victory for two reasons: their righteousness, and the nations' wickedness. A kind of simple binary logic. Who won? We did. So who is righteous? We are. And who is wicked? They are. This turns the whole story of the conquest into a cowboy western, where it is very clear-cut who are the goodies and who are the baddies. However, Moses challenges this simplistic equation, denying one part of it and affirming the other. It was true that God was judging the Canaanites for their wickedness. But it was *not* true that the Israelites could therefore conclude that they themselves were righteous.

Moses reinforces this by declaring in 9:5 that God gave Israel the victory not merely because of the enemy's wickedness, but because of God's own faithfulness to what he swore to Abraham and Jacob. He had made a promise to give Israel this land, and he was going to keep it. If it had depended on their righteousness, they would have won no victories at all; those victories were won not because of Israel's righteousness but in spite of their stubbornness. Verse 6 finishes, '. . . God is giving you this good land to possess, [even though] you are a stiff-necked people.' It was only by God's grace that they had got this far.

What do these verses say to us? Theologically, they stand with the rest of the Scriptures in affirming the grace of God and denying that any human claim upon God arises out of our own righteousness. Israel wanted to boast, and God told them they had nothing to boast about. We may compare this to Romans 3, where Paul asks whether, through the enormous privilege of having received God's revelation and God's covenant, the people of Israel are thereby made morally superior to the Gentiles. His answer is, no, they are not. In Romans 3:1 he asks, 'What advantage, then, is there in being a Jew, or what value is there in circumcision?' And he answers, 'Much in every way! First of all, they have been entrusted with the very words of God' (3:2). But then he says, 'What shall we conclude then? Are we [Jews] any better? Not at all! We have already made the charge that Jews and Gentiles alike are all under sin. As it is written: "There is no-one righteous not even one; there is no-one who understands, no-one who seeks God"' (3:9–11). And then comes the famous verse: 'There is no difference, for all have sinned and fall short of the glory of God . . .' (3:23). Whether you are a Jew or a Gentile, all stand on the same level before God as sinners, stiff-necked, stubborn and rebellious.

God wants to make sure that those he has redeemed and enables to be victorious – in Old Testament or New Testament terms – do not begin to acquire the glow of pride and self-congratulation which would lead us to think God is being good to us because of some quality that we have. It is by God's grace and nothing else that we stand redeemed and victorious.

The justice of the conquest

Secondly, there is the problem of the conquest. God sent the Israelites into Canaan to attack the civilization dwelling in that land, to destroy its peoples and communities and religion. Wherever the Old Testament is taught, questions like this arise: how can we square God's commands to destroy the Canaanites with our belief in God's love? Deuteronomy 9 helps to put that problem in perspective, though it may not answer our questions completely. It places the conquest of Canaan in the moral framework of an act of God's justice and judgment against the Canaanites' wickedness. Here God exercised his sovereign, righteous, providential rule within history.

It is the consistent view of the Old Testament,

echoed in the book of Hebrews and elsewhere in the New Testament, that the judgment of the Canaanites was for their wickedness. The first indication of this is in Genesis 15, where God, having renewed his covenant promise to Abraham to bless him and make him a great nation, told him that his descendants would go down into a country where they would be enslaved for generations. Then, according to Genesis 15:16, God said, 'In the fourth generation your descendants will come back here [to Canaan], for the sin of the Amorites has not yet reached its full measure.' The Amorites who dwelt in Canaan had not yet attained the level of wickedness that would justify God's acting against them, but a day would come when their society would be so polluted, callous and unjust that God's judgment and destruction of them would be just.

This theme becomes more explicit in Leviticus. Leviticus 18 gives a long list of the sins Israel were commanded not to commit – all kinds of perversion and immorality, including child sacrifice – and concludes,

Do not defile yourselves in any of these ways, because this is how the nations that I am going to drive out before you became defiled. Even the land was defiled; so I punished it for its sin, and the land vomited out its inhabitants. But you must keep my decrees and my laws. The native-born and the aliens living among you must not do any of these detestable things, for all these things were done by the people who lived in the land before you, and the land became defiled (18:24).

Similarly in Leviticus 20:

Keep all my decrees and laws and follow them, so that the land where I am bringing you to live may not vomit you out. You must not live according to the customs of the nations I am going to drive out before you. Because they did all these things, I abhorred them (20:22–24).

It is clear from all this that the endemic sin of the Canaanites was the moral reason for which God acted in judgment against them. It was not a matter of arbitrary violence but of deserved punishment.

A God without favourites

Another point, often overlooked, is that in the same texts in which God declares his intention of driving out the Canaanites because of their wickedness, he also tells the Israelites that if they behave in the same way, he will drive them out of the land too. If his people went the way of sin and wickedness, idolatry and immorality, God would bring upon them exactly the same judgment as he brought against the Canaanites. And that is exactly what happened in Israel's later history. God does not have favourites. The conquest was not a matter of God favouring the nation he happened to like more. God is a consistent God, who keeps his promises and his threats to all nations of the world in his acts of sovereign judgment.

However, the main point being made to the Israelites was that the wickedness of the Canaanites did not establish the righteousness of Israel. In warfare, both ancient and modern, it is tempting to assume that whoever wins is in the right and whoever loses is in the wrong: God will smile on the righteous and judge the wicked. According to Deuteronomy 9, that is not the case. God can even use those who are far from righteous in order to bring about his acts of judgment and justice in the history of the world. Canaanite wickedness did not make the Israelites righteous, and God's use of Israel as an agent of his judgment was not premised on their being more righteous than other nations.

We should bear this perspective in mind when we look at recent history. One of the most sickening aspects of the Gulf War, after the horror of what happened, the appalling bloodshed and destruction, was the way the victors basked in self-righteousness. They presented themselves as the defenders of the right, the good and the free against the forces of evil represented by the enemy. But what needed to be said was that the outcome of the war, in so far as it represented any kind of justice at all, came not from their righteousness but from God's sovereign acts within history.

Judgment of God's people

Remember this and never forget how you provoked the LORD your God to anger in the desert. From the day you left Egypt until you arrived here, you have been rebellious against the LORD. At Horeb you aroused the

LORD's wrath so that he was angry enough to destroy you. When I went up on the mountain to receive the tablets of stone, tablets of the covenant that the LORD had made with you, I stayed on the mountain forty days and forty nights; I ate no bread and drank no water. The LORD gave me two stone tablets inscribed by the finger of God. On them were all the commandments the LORD proclaimed to you on the mountain out of the fire, on the day of the assembly.

At the end of the forty days and forty nights, the LORD gave me the two stone tablets, the tablets of the covenant. Then the LORD told me, 'Go down from here at once, because your people whom you brought out of Egypt have become corrupt. They have turned away quickly from what I commanded them and have made a cast idol for themselves.'

And the LORD said to me, 'I have seen this people, and they are a stiff-necked people indeed! Let me alone, so that I may destroy them and blot out their name from under heaven. And I will make you into a nation stronger and more numerous than they.'

So I turned and went down from the

mountain while it was ablaze with fire. And the two tablets of the covenant were in my hands. When I looked, I saw that you had sinned against the LORD your God; you had made for yourselves an idol cast in the shape of a calf. You had turned aside quickly from the way that the LORD had commanded you. So I took the two tablets and threw them out of my hands, breaking them to pieces before your eyes.

Then once again I fell prostrate before the LORD for forty days and forty nights; I ate no bread and drank no water, because of all the sin you had committed, doing what was evil in the LORD's sight and so provoking him to anger. I feared the anger and wrath of the LORD, for he was angry enough with you to destroy you. But again the LORD listened to me. And the LORD was angry enough with Aaron to destroy him, but at that time I prayed for Aaron too. Also I took that sinful thing of yours, the calf you had made, and burned it in the fire. Then I crushed it and ground it to powder as fine as dust and threw the dust into a stream that flowed down the mountain.

You also made the LORD angry at Taberah, at Massah and at Kibroth Hattaavah.

And when the LORD sent you out from Kadesh Barnea, he said, 'Go up and take possession of the land I have given you.' But you rebelled against the command of the LORD your God. You did not trust him or obey him. You have been rebellious against the LORD ever since I have known you (9:7–24).

The theme of Deuteronomy 9 is to undermine Israel's temptation to arrogance and self-right-eousness. Following the declaration that God gives them victory over other nations because of the wickedness of those other nations, one might expect Moses to give some examples of that wickedness. Later on, in chapter 12 he does describe something of the horror of Canaanite civilization: 'You must not worship the LORD your God in their way, because in worshipping their gods, they do all kinds of detestable things the LORD hates. They even burn their sons and daughters in the fire as sacrifices to their gods' (12:31). But in chapter 9, instead of cataloguing the wickedness of *other nations*, Moses presents a catalogue of the failures of *God's own people*, and of God's acts of judgment upon them. He says, 'From the day you left Egypt until you arrived here, you have been rebellious against the LORD' (9:7). And, 'You have been rebellious against the LORD ever since I have known you' (9:24). Moses does not pull his punches. He wants the Israelites to be aware of their own history, and what it means that they remain the people of God in spite of that history.

The main example given of Israel's failure is the great rebellion that took place at Mount Sinai. But Moses pauses in describing that event to remark, 'You also made the LORD angry at Taberah, at Massah and at Kibroth Hattaavah. And when the LORD sent you out from Kadesh Barnea, he said, "Go up and take possession of the land I have given you." But you rebelled against the command of the LORD your god. You did not trust him or obey him' (9:22–23). In other words, Moses could have chosen any number of occasions to illustrate Israel's rebellion and wickedness.

Israel's apostasy

Let us examine the rebellion at Mount Sinai (Horeb). Deuteronomy 9:8 says, 'At Horeb you aroused the LORD's wrath so that he was angry enough to destroy you.' Strong words. The word for 'destroy' is exactly the same as that used in verse 3 to describe what God was going to do to the Canaanite nations. Moses reminds the Israelites that there had been an occasion when God was so angry with *them* that he was ready to destroy *them*. Again, this deflates any arrogance regarding the conquest. It was only by grace that Israel had survived to this point.

The account from verse 9 onwards is a retelling of the great apostasy of the golden calf in Exodus 32 – 34. Moses had gone up the mountain to receive the Ten Commandments. Meanwhile the people down below, losing their trust in Moses during his absence, asked Aaron to do something to help them. So Aaron had them hand over their earrings and their gold and from these he fashioned a golden calf – although when Moses returned and asked for an explanation, Aaron said they had simply thrown the gold into the fire and out had come the golden calf. Once the idol was made, the people not only bowed down and worshipped it, but fell into carousing and immorality. It was a monumental act of apostasy and sin.

God's anger

God was so angry that he nearly repudiated the

Sinai covenant. He was on the verge of telling this people – to whom he had said at Sinai, 'You will be my people and I will be your God' – that they were *not* now his people. I am reminded of the sad little son of Hosea who was named Lo-Ammi, which translates as 'Not Mine', and the daughter Lo-Ruhamah, whose name means 'Not Loved'. Hosea had to give his children such terrible names as prophetic signs that that was how God felt about Israel – no longer the covenant people.

Moses' breaking of the tablets on which the Ten Commandments were inscribed made it clear that the Sinai covenant had been broken. Moses did not just drop them because he was shocked. He threw them down before the eyes of the people, as if to declare that the covenant was broken – God was rejecting them as his people.

But worse was to come. In 9:13, God says to Moses, 'I have seen this people, and they are a stiff-necked people indeed! Let me alone, so that I may destroy them and blot out their name from under heaven. And I will make you into a nation stronger and more numerous than they.' Exodus 32:10 is even stronger: 'Now leave me alone so that my anger may burn against them and that I may destroy them. Then I will make you into a great nation.' This is a clear echo of the covenant with Abraham. God had promised Abraham that he would make him into a great nation. Now he was saying the same thing to Moses. He would wipe out the people of Abraham and start again with Moses, to create the people of Moses. Some commentators suggest an echo of the flood: God was prepared to destroy the whole of this people and start again with one man as he had done with Noah. The anger of God is terrifying; Moses must have trembled to hear these words.

It is important that we hold on to the wonderful biblical truths about God's assurance that once we are his people we will always be his people, and of his faithfulness and mercy and grace, which will see us through to the end. But that should never make us complacent about sin and idolatry among the people of God. We should take seriously the biblical teaching about the anger of God, even towards his own people. Remember the warnings of Jesus to people who would call him 'Lord' but to whom he would say on the day of judgment, 'I never knew you. Away from me, you evildoers!' (Matthew 7:23). Remember the warnings in Hebrews about how terrible it is for those who have once known the living God to fall into his hands (Hebrews 10:26–31). Difficult scriptures. Theologians puzzle over them. But the truth is that sin is to be judged, and sin among the people of God brings God's anger. This speaks to any who take the view that if God has saved them and they are assured of a place in heaven, then why should they not sin (*cf.* Romans 6:1ff.).

After destroying the tablets, Moses took the golden calf, burned it in the fire, and ground it to dust, which he then threw away. Another account tells us that the dust was put in the water and the people made to drink it (Exodus 32:20). Thus the act of idolatry itself was destroyed.

Moses' intercession

I lay prostrate before the LORD those forty days and forty nights because the LORD had said he would destroy you. I prayed to the LORD and said, 'O Sovereign LORD, do not destroy your people, your own inheritance that you redeemed by your great power and brought out of Egypt with a mighty hand. Remember your servants Abraham, Isaac and

3 Confronting God **85**

Jacob. Overlook the stubbornness of this people, their wickedness and their sin. Otherwise, the country from which you brought us will say, "Because the LORD was not able to take them into the land he had promised them, and because he hated them, he brought them out to put them to death in the desert." But they are your people, your inheritance that you brought out by your great power and your outstretched arm' (9:25–29).

Here in Deuteronomy 9:25–29, as in Exodus 32 – 33, comes Moses' amazing intercession. God had threatened to renounce the Sinai covenant and the covenant with Abraham and to start again with Moses. With astonishing boldness, Moses puts up his hand to God and comes as close as we can imagine to rebuking God. Moses, we are told, was closer to the heart of God than any other human being. He was the humble friend and servant of the Lord, he spoke with the Lord face to face, and he was able to speak to God like this. But, still, it is amazing.

Think of the temptation God was putting before Moses. God was telling him he could be his new Abraham. The future people of God would be called the children of Moses, not the

children of Abraham or the children of Israel.
Think how Moses felt, having struggled with
these people who had been grumbly and
rebellious the whole time he had led them, now
suddenly faced with the prospect that God
would dispose of them and start afresh with
him. Many Christian ministers have faced a
temptation like that. You have a tough time in a
particular church. What is the easiest thing to
do? Get up and go. Start a para-church ministry
where you can be your own boss. Here we see
Moses as not only the model intercessor for his
people but also the model leader of God's
people. He was committed to them. Instead of
being tempted by the thought that God would
destroy these rebels and start again with him, he
asks God how he could even think of treating
his own people thus.

God's commitment

In his prayer of intercession, Moses first brings
to God's attention the Sinai covenant which
God appeared to be renouncing.

I lay prostrate before the LORD those forty
days and forty nights because the LORD had

said he would destroy you. I prayed to the
LORD and said, 'O Sovereign LORD, do not
destroy your people, your own inheritance
that you redeemed by your great power and
brought out of Egypt with a mighty hand'
(9:25–26).

Then Moses continues, '. . . they are *your*
people, *your* inheritance that *you* brought out
by your great power and your outstretched arm'
(9:29). This is a deliberate echo of 9:12. God had
in effect said to Moses, 'Look what *your* people
whom *you* brought out of Egypt are doing.' And
now Moses is saying to God, 'This is your people
and you brought them out of Egypt.' Moses had
not wanted the job of leading the Israelites out of
captivity. So he protests to God that it was not
himself who had brought the people out of
Egypt, but God. How bold he is. When God
says 'your people, Moses', Moses says 'no, your
people, God'. He reflects to God's heart the
ultimate truth that God is committed to his
people. If God has said 'You shall be my people',
then God cannot go back on his word. They are
God's people because God called them his
people. And so Moses asks God to remain
committed to them and not to destroy them.

God's existence

In response to God's promise that he will make him into a great nation (9:14), Moses replies with indignation: 'Remember your servants Abraham, Isaac and Jacob' (9:27). Moses is most daring of all when he reminds God of his covenant with Abraham. Genesis 15 describes God's oath to Abraham, when Abraham had carried out the sacrificial ritual of covenant. This involved cutting some animals in half and then walking between the severed parts of the animals to seal the solemn promise. This ritual set up a powerful self-curse. The symbolism was that if you broke your word and failed to keep your promise, then you would be like these animals, cut up and dead. God, as Hebrews tells us, swore on his very self that he would keep his promise to Abraham. There was nothing higher that he could swear by. God was covenanting on his own existence that he would be faithful to Abraham, his people, and his purposes through Abraham. And so Moses was asking God what it would mean for God himself if he were to destroy his people. Because God had sworn to be faithful to Abraham, he could not destroy Abraham's children finally and for ever. He could judge them or punish them, but he could not abandon his promise to Abraham without breaking his own oath and denying his own being and existence.

God's reputation

This leads to a third aspect of Moses' intercession. He appeals to God's own reputation:

> Overlook the stubbornness of this people, their wickedness and their sin. Otherwise, the country from which you brought us will say, 'Because the LORD was not able to take them into the land he had promised them, and because he hated them, he brought them out to put them to death in the desert' (9:27–28).

If God, having brought the Israelites all this way, were suddenly to destroy them, what would the Egyptians think? They would say that Yahweh, the God of Israel, was inconsistent, that he did not know what he was doing, that he saved people only to kill them. This was expressed even more strongly on another occasion of Moses' intercession, when God was threatening to destroy the Israelites because of their failure to enter the promised land. Numbers 14 relates,

> Moses said to the LORD, 'Then the Egyptians will hear about it! By your power you brought these people up from among them. And they will tell the inhabitants of this land about it. They have already heard that you, O LORD, are with these people and that you, O LORD, have been seen face to face, that your cloud stays over them, and that you go before them in a pillar of cloud by day and a pillar of fire by night. If you put these people to death all at one time, the nations who have heard this report about you will say, "The LORD was not able to bring these people into the land he promised them on oath; so he slaughtered them in the desert" ' (Numbers 14:13–16).

On both occasions, Moses asked God to think about what people would say about him as God if he carried out his threat to his people. We know from the rest of the Scriptures that God is concerned about his name, not in the childish way that we might be, but concerned as the creator of the universe for the holiness of his name and for what the nations of the world think of him.

As in all good intercessory prayer, Moses went to the heart of God's own priorities. In Deuteronomy 9 he says, '. . . the LORD listened to me' (9:19). And again in the next chapters, '. . . the LORD listened to me at this time also. It was not his will to destroy you' (10:10). God listened to Moses because Moses pleaded with him for the sake of three things precious to God's heart: his love for his people, his faithfulness to his promise, his concern for his name. This model of intercession is echoed in other parts of the Old Testament, such as the great prayer of Daniel in Daniel 9, and the prayer of Nehemiah in Nehemiah 9. Dial 999 for intercessory prayer: Deuteronomy 9, Nehemiah 9, Daniel 9! All three men, Moses, Daniel and Nehemiah, knew how to touch God's heart because they knew what was most important to God himself. This is how we too should frame our prayers of intercession.

The breach in God's heart and human intercession

There remains, however, a mystery to this disturbing text. It raises certain questions. Was

God really serious? What would have happened if Moses had tripped up going down the mountain, and, being concussed, had been unable to pray? Had God really forgotten the things that Moses reminded him of? Many questions come to mind around the experience of intercessory prayer. Why does not God simply do what he wants to do? Why does he want us to intercede in prayer?

It is important to treat a text like Deuteronomy 9 with integrity, to regard it as a genuine encounter between Moses and the living God, with no play acting. Psalm 106:23 tells us that God would have destroyed his people if Moses had not interceded. God was not bluffing, and Moses did not think that God was bluffing. Moses took God seriously, but he presented to God some things that God took even more seriously: his people, his promise and his name.

We could say that Moses was trying to change God's mind. At the same time, he was appealing to God to be consistent. He was asking God to change his immediate intention in order to be faithful to his long-term goals.

It appears that God wanted Moses to do that. There is a mystery in the little expression God addresses to Moses: 'Let me alone' (9:13).

Jewish commentators down the centuries have seen something very profound in that moment. If God had said to Moses, 'Let me alone', Moses must have already begun to protest. Why did God need to say that? He could have destroyed the people immediately without telling Moses. It seems that he declared his intention to Moses and then said, 'Let me alone', in the hope that Moses would come back and *not* let him alone. God was inviting Moses' intercession into his own deliberation, as he had done with Abraham immediately before the destruction of Sodom and Gomorrah. In Genesis 18, God went and had a meal with Abraham and Sarah, bringing two of his angels who were on the way to Sodom and Gomorrah. God wondered whether to hide from Abraham what he was about to do, and decided not to. Abraham, having heard God's intention, interceded on behalf of the wicked. It appears that God chooses to bring our prayers into his own deliberation. Our intercession is not an irritating interruption in God's purpose; it is an integral part of the way he exercises his sovereignty in history.

One commentator, B. S. Childs, expresses it like this:

God vows the most severe punishment imaginable. But then suddenly he conditions it, as it were, on Moses' agreement. 'Let me alone, that I may consume them.' The effect is that God himself leaves the door open for intercession. He allows himself to be persuaded. That is what a mediator is for (*The Book of Exodus*, Westminster, 1974, p. 567).

Another commentator, Terence Fretheim, writes,

While these ought not to be considered arguments that God had not thought of before, to have them articulated in such a forceful way by one who has been invited into the deliberation regarding Israel's future, gives them a new status. That is, God takes Moses' contribution with the utmost seriousness; God's acquiescence to the arguments indicates that God treats the conversation with Moses with integrity and honours his human insight as an important ingredient in the shaping of the future. If Moses thinks these things, then they take on a significance, [even to the mind and heart of God] (*The Suffering of God*, Fortress, 1985, pp. 50f.).

Moses was not so much arguing *against* God as participating in an argument *within* God. There was a tension in God's relationship with this rebellious people whom he loved but was angry with. Moses entered that breach in the heart of God with his prayers. That insight should encourage us as we in turn intercede with God for his world and his people.

This chapter of Deuteronomy has exposed us to the awful seriousness of God's wrath and judgment. How should we respond to those terrifying words about the judgment of God on the wicked and on his own people? As we learned in the first part of chapter 9, we must avoid any feeling of self-righteousness when God judges the wicked. Rather, we should recognize our own failings, and remember, 'There but for the grace of God go I.' And when we are faced with the judgment of God upon his people, we should engage in intercessory prayer, not to try and persuade a reluctant God to change his mind, but rather to enter the deepest concerns of God's own heart for his people, his promises, his name and his glory.

Imitating God

(Deuteronomy 10:12–22)

And now, O Israel, what does the LORD your God ask of you but to fear the LORD your God, to walk in all his ways, to love him, to serve the LORD your God with all your heart and with all your soul, and to observe the LORD's commands and decrees that I am giving you today for your own good?

To the LORD your God belong the heavens, even the highest heavens, the earth and everything in it. Yet the LORD set his affection on your forefathers and loved them, and he chose you, their descendants, above all the nations, as it is today. Circumcise your hearts, therefore, and do not be stiff-necked any longer. For the LORD your God is God of gods and Lord of lords, the great God, mighty and awesome, who shows no partiality and accepts no bribes. He defends the cause of the fatherless and the widow, and loves the alien, giving him food and clothing. And you are to love those who are aliens, for you yourselves were aliens in Egypt. Fear the LORD your God and serve him. Hold fast to him and take your oaths in his name. He is your praise; he is your God, who performed for you those great and awesome wonders you saw with your own eyes. Your fore-fathers who went down into Egypt were seventy in all, and now the LORD your God has made you as numerous as the stars in the sky (10:12–22).

A five-note opening chord

This passage is one of my favourites in the Old Testament. It is rich with wisdom and insight. The first section (10:12–13) is like a great opening chord, in which there are five separate notes and yet they all ring together in harmony.

Moses is building up towards the climax of the opening section of the book of Deuteronomy. The climax comes in chapter 11, when he challenges the people to choose life and blessing rather than death. His 'And now, O Israel . . .' in verse 12 is like the 'And finally . . .' of a great sermon, or the 'Therefore . . .' in some of Paul's letters (for example, in Romans 12 and Ephesians 4) – a transition from great teaching about what God has done for us in the past, through to a statement of what God requires of us in response.

In chapter 9 we saw the great apostasy of the Israelites at Mount Sinai, and how, through the intercession of Moses, God was merciful to his people and spared them instead of destroying them. His amazing forgiveness is described in 10:10: '. . . the LORD listened to me . . . It was not his will to destroy you.' And thus God commanded Moses to lead the people onward in his presence. Such mercy and forgiveness inevitably creates a corresponding 'Therefore . . .'

Simple obedience

What does God require of us in response to his loving mercy? What he asks is that we fear him, walk in his ways, love him, serve him and obey him. Five notes. We shall consider each of these, but the essence of what Moses is saying here is that obedience is fundamentally simple. Not simple in the sense of 'easy'. If obedience to God were easy, there would be no need for a book like Deuteronomy; there would be no need for all this exhortation. But obedience is essentially straightforward.

First, it is simple because there is only one God. Monotheism is a liberating faith. If you have lots of gods in your religion, then you have problems. You can never be sure whether in obeying one god you might be displeasing another. So polytheistic religion, with many competing gods and goddesses, is often morally confused, whereas biblical faith has moral simplicity because there is only one God to please and to obey. If you do what pleases him, then you will be doing what is right.

Secondly, obedience is also simple because this one living God has gone to great pains to make his will clear to us. In the fundamentals of life, we do not have to grope around in the darkness wondering what we should do. In Deuteronomy 30:11–12, towards the second great climax of the book, Moses says to the people of Israel, 'Now what I am commanding you today is not too difficult for you or beyond your reach. It is not up in heaven, so that you have to ask, "Who will ascend into heaven to get it and proclaim it to us that we may obey it?"' Ultimately, we have no need of religious experts who will somehow obtain the word of God and find out what God's will for us is. 'The word [of God] is very near you; it is in your mouth and in your heart' (30:14). God gave us his word and his law so that we could obey it.

One distorted view of the Old Testament law says that God gave us his law as a standard of conduct we could never hope to achieve, so that it would drive us despairing to our knees and eventually to the gospel. There is an element of truth in that. The premise of the gospel is that, being fallen and sinful, we cannot ultimately obey God and keep his law. But that is not because God's law was devised as something we could never fulfil. The Psalms and other parts of the Old Testament rejoice in the fact that God has revealed to us his will and his word, so that we can know how we ought to live and then set out to obey God and, doing that, to know him.

Obedience is simple because God has made his will clear. As the prophet Micah says, 'He has showed you, O man, what is good. And what does the LORD require of you? To act justly and to love mercy and to walk humbly with your God' (Micah 6:8).

This is all that really matters. Do you fear God? Do you want to walk in his ways? Do you love him? Do you want to serve him? Do you desire to obey him? That is what God is looking for. Not 'Can you sign every basis of faith that anybody lays before you?' – although it is important that we understand the central truths of our faith and can assent to them with our minds. Not 'Can you be sure that your worship is exactly the way this person or denomination says?' – although it is important that our worship is truthful, biblical and pleasing to God. Not 'Have you got an answer to every question or a solution to every problem?' – although it is important that we wrestle with the great questions of life. One of the tragic causes of division among the people of God is that we have so often insisted on asking of people more than God himself asks of people. What God wants is the humble, obedient love of our hearts.

Fear the Lord your God

To fear God does not mean to be terrified of him, although, in the context of sin and rebellion, there is a place for being afraid of God, as chapter 9 reminded us. In 10:12, to fear God means to take him seriously, to give him the honour and respect that are due him because he is God.

Deuteronomy 5:29 contains a lovely expression of God's longing for his people. At the time when the Ten Commandments were given, the people were so afraid of God and what was happening on Mount Sinai that they told Moses to go up the mountain and hear what God had to say; meanwhile they would wait at the bottom till he came back. God, sensing the awe and reverence in their hearts, said, 'Oh, that their hearts would be inclined to fear me and keep all my commands always . . .' We sense God's wistfulness, for he knew that they would not do as he wished them to.

The wisdom books of the Old Testament tell us that fear of the Lord is the beginning of wisdom. The first principle of wise living is to put God first and take him seriously. Conversely, the essence of folly is to ignore God. If you do not fear God, you can be very clever and yet an utter fool.

Walk in all his ways

We should watch the way that God moves, and then follow in his footsteps. As one of our older hymns says, 'O let me see thy footprints, and in them plant my own' (see 'O Jesus, I have promised to serve thee to the end'). And in Deuteronomy 5:32–33, we read, 'So be careful to do what the LORD your God has commanded you; do not turn aside to the right or to the left. Walk in all the ways that the LORD your God has commanded you . . .' Do not wander off down some attractive byway, but follow God.

The expression 'walking in the ways of the Lord' is the nearest biblical equivalent of what we might call 'Old Testament ethics'. It means to follow God's character. The ways of the Lord are the ethics he commands us to live by. In Genesis 18:19 God reflects upon his calling of Abraham: 'For I have chosen him, so that he will direct his children and his household after him to keep the way of the LORD by doing what is right and just . . .' God wanted a people who would walk in his ways by living in righteousness and justice, in a world that was walking in the ways of Sodom.

Love the Lord your God

In any group of five, there is always a middle one. The central note of the five notes in Deuteronomy 10:12–13 is 'love'. This text reminds me of one of my favourite styles of piano playing: the gentle country style associated with Floyd Cramer and Ched Atkins, where the melody is somewhere in the middle of the notes you play, dressed up with a flavouring of other notes above and below. The real heart of these two verses is 'Love the LORD your God with all your heart and with all your soul and with all your strength.' This is the first and greatest commandment, which we examined fully in chapter 2.

Serve the Lord your God

The word used for 'serve' is a strong one; it connotes bonded service and slavery. It is the word used in reference to Israel serving Pharaoh in Egypt. So intolerable was that situation to God that he had sent Moses to tell Pharaoh,

'Israel is my first-born son' (Exodus 4:22). The Israelites should not have been serving Pharaoh, but serving God. So God had commanded Pharaoh, 'Let my son go, so that he may [serve me and] worship me' (Exodus 4:23; the one Hebrew verb has the double meaning of 'serve' and 'worship').

These people whom God had redeemed and brought to himself were now told that their highest purpose was to *serve* him (Deuteronomy 10:12). To serve someone implies lowliness and humility, but at the same time there is no higher honour than to be called the servant of the Lord. Very few people in the Old Testament were given the title 'servant of the Lord'. Moses was one of them. Later on, in the book of Isaiah, the same title was applied to the one who would be in perfect obedience to God, who would bring Israel back to God and bring the light of God's salvation to the ends of the world – the servant of God.

Observe the Lord's commands

The term used here expresses careful, conscientious attention to what God says. It is akin to the language parents might use when they want children to be sure they have understood where they have to go and how to get home. It evokes the manner in which Jesus told his disciples that they were to go and make disciples of all nations, baptizing them and teaching them to observe 'everything I have commanded you' (Matthew 28:20). That last phrase might have come straight from Deuteronomy. We are to be disciples who make disciples and lead others to be obedient in serving God and keeping his commandments, as we ourselves are trying to do.

The simplicity, singleness and wholeness of this chord of five notes is beautiful. What else matters in life except to fear God, to walk in his ways, to love him, to serve him and to obey him?

For your own good

Finally, notice the motivation for doing these things: '. . . for your own good' (10:13). People sometimes think that the purpose of obeying God's law is simply to keep him happy. It is true that he is pleased when we keep his law, but the reason why God gave us his law is not for his good, it is for our good. This is the God who is the creator of human life, the God who knows what is best for his people and for all people. The Ten Commandments are often described as the Maker's instructions – for how human life will function best. Life is most fulfilled and happy when we keep God's law.

In the Old Testament, obedience to God is never presented as a burden or as something we have to struggle with in order to achieve salvation. Quite the contrary. In the Psalms the law is described as one of the best gifts of God's loving grace. It is something precious.

> Blessed is the man
>   who does not walk in the counsel of the
>   wicked
> or stand in the way of sinners . . .
> But his delight is in the law of the LORD,
>   and on his law he meditates day and night.
> He is like a tree planted by streams of water,
>   which yields its fruit in season . . .
>   (Psalm 1:1–3)

Psalm 19 describes the law of the Lord as sweeter than honey and more precious than gold. That is not the language of someone sweating away under the burden of legalism; it is the language of someone who has discovered in God's law something infinitely precious and good. In Psalm 119 the law is described using many different metaphors. It is light, it is a lamp, it is food, it is water, it is life, it is the gift of God's grace. It is tragic when Christians turn obedience into dreary bondage, or, conversely, when people say that biblical morality is too narrow and contrary to our best interests. God tells us to love him, fear him, serve him, obey him – for our own good.

A double three-part symphony

Continuing the musical metaphor, I would describe the second part of this passage (10:14– 19) as a double three-part surprise symphony. In studying the Bible we should pay attention to form as well as content. This is sometimes called a literary approach. Reading the text as literature, you see how it is put together and how the writer has shaped it into an aesthetic pattern.

The pattern in this section consists of two sequences of three verses. In verses 14 and 17 there is a hymnlike expression of praise. 'To the LORD your God belong the heavens, even the highest heavens, the earth and everything in it'

(10:14). You can hear the music flooding in as a choir prepares to sing that. And then that mood returns: 'For the LORD your God is God of gods and Lord of lords . . .' (10:17). You can almost hear the orchestra tuning up for Handel's *Messiah*. Each of these two verses is followed by something that might seem surprising after such great truths about God. Verse 15 says that God 'set his affection on your forefathers and loved them'. And in verse 18 this great God defends the cause of the orphan, the widow and the stranger. Then, after each of those verses comes the response that we should make. So the sequence is: praise of what God is like (verses 14, 17); something surprising (verses 15, 18); our required response (verses 16, 19).

Universal ownership

'To the LORD your God belong the heavens, even the highest heavens, the earth and everything in it' (10:14). This is the most astounding claim one can imagine, especially when you remember it is being made by Moses on behalf of a bunch of second-generation escaped slaves from the Egyptian empire. The people of Israel were never a great nation. They achieved a miniature empire at the time of David and Solomon, but for most of their history they were a minor nation among the great empires of the ancient Near East. Yet here Moses was proclaiming that their God, Yahweh, was the owner of the whole of the heavens and the whole of the earth. The same claim is made in the Psalms. For example, Psalm 24 begins, 'The earth is the LORD's, and everything in it . . .' And Psalm 95 says:

> For the LORD is the great God,
>   the great King above all gods.
> In his hand are the depths of the earth,
>   and the mountain peaks belong to him.
> The sea is his, for he made it,
>   and his hands formed the dry land.
>
> (Psalm 95:3–5)

The world belongs to God, because he made it. There is absolutely nothing in creation, in the highest heavens or the deepest earth, that does not belong to God.

And yet some of the commentaries on Deuteronomy say, in one way or another, that this claim was only with respect to Israel and did not constitute true monotheism; that the

Israelites claimed merely that Yahweh had authority over them and so *they* would worship only him. It is hard to understand how commentators can believe this. If absolutely everything in heaven and on earth belongs to Yahweh, that does not leave very much to belong to any other god!

It also challenges evangelical Christians to be careful not to slip into a dualism in which we have our God for all the nice things and a rather different god – Satan we might call him – for everything nasty. I do not deny the reality of evil and of Satan and his kingdom, but there is a Christian misunderstanding of such things which leads to a dualistic view of God and Satan which this text will not allow. Everything in heaven and on earth belongs to God. Satan is only an angel, a part of creation. We should never flatter him by treating him as a rival god. He has no *divine* power.

One ethical implication of all this is that if the whole of the earth belongs to God, then it does not belong to us. God is the landlord. We are tenants, stewards, accountable to God for how we use the resources of the earth, the land and the sea and all that is in them, and for our attitude to other people, to ourselves and to our sexuality. One of the most important principles of a biblical approach to ethics is that everything belongs to God.

Another important implication is for Christian mission. There is no part of this world that does not belong to God and, in New Testament terms as affirmed in Colossians, to Christ. There is no such thing as a godless place. When, in Matthew 28, Jesus stood on the Mount of Ascension and told his disciples to go and make disciples of the nations, what right had he to say that and what right have we to do it? What right have we to go to people anywhere on earth and say, 'You must worship the Lord; you must become a Christian; you must submit to Christ; you must accept Jesus as Lord?' We have no right, except that the earth is the Lord's and everything in it. Jesus prefaced that command 'go and make disciples' with the statement, 'All authority in heaven and on earth is given to me.' That is his ownership expressed as the foundation of Christian mission, using the language that Deuteronomy used of Yahweh.

Let us never downplay that incredible statement, 'To the LORD your God belong the heavens, even the highest heavens, the earth and everything in it.' Let us allow our hearts and minds to be filled with the wonder of that, especially when we look up at the stars and see the vastness of creation.

A surprising choice

Even in the Hebrew, the word 'yet' that introduces 10:15 has the nuance of introducing a surprise. In spite of his cosmic ownership of the whole of creation, 'the LORD set his affection on your forefathers and loved them, and he chose you, their descendants, above all the nations, as it is today'. A more accurate translation of 'above all the nations' would be 'from all the nations'. The surprise is that, despite his universal sovereignty, God chose to focus his love on the small group of people who became the ancestors of Israel. As Deuteronomy 7 emphasizes, 'The LORD did not set his affection on you and choose you because you were more numerous than other peoples, for you were the fewest of all peoples' (7:7). Whether we look at it from the point of view of God's greatness or Israel's smallness, the choice that God made is surprising.

It is important to understand verses 14 and 15

in the light of each other. Otherwise the affirmations they make can get separated and used wrongly. We should recognize that it is the God of universal sovereignty who has made this specific choice of Israel and, through Israel, of the whole people of God of which we ourselves are part. The ownership is universal but the election is particular. But we should also remember that the God who loved, chose, called and saved Israel is the God who owns the whole world. There are tendencies in some forms of Christian theology to go to one extreme or the other. Some people so want to express God's universality that God becomes the God of everybody; this results in a universalism in which there is no difference between one religion and another, between the people of God and other people, or between the God of Israel and any other god. This is unbiblical. God has chosen the particular historical people of Israel, brought Jesus to the world through them, and committed himself to us his people.

The other danger is to emphasize so much the biblical doctrine of election – that we are the people who have come to God because of God's call and choice – that one ends up with a narrow, sectarian exclusivism which loses touch with the fact that the God we are privileged to know in Christ, the God who has called and chosen us in Christ, is also the God of the universe, to whom everything belongs.

Circumcise your hearts

You might expect that such a statement of God's love for his people would be followed by some comforting affirmation that they should therefore rejoice and praise him. There are places in the book of Psalms where God's choice and love of Israel are made the basis for worship and rejoicing. But in the context of Deuteronomy, Moses is anxious to extinguish among the Israelites any form of self-congratulation about their status as God's chosen people. So, instead of telling them to be glad, he tells them they must circumcise their hearts and be stiff-necked no longer. They should repent and remember their history. Similarly God spoke through Amos the shocking words 'You only have I chosen . . . therefore I will punish you . . .' (Amos 3:2).

Those elected to be God's people have the responsibility of humbling themselves before him, of being obedient to him through the circumcision of their hearts. Paul was not the first to teach that we must circumcise our hearts. Physical circumcision was the sign of belonging to the covenant people of God, with all the commitment to obedient, loyal response that went with it. 'Circumcision of the heart' meant that what was a physical symbol should be a practical reality in life – true submission to God and willing obedience.

Universal sovereignty

In the second half of the symphony, the music returns in Deuteronomy 10:17 – 'For the LORD your God is God of gods and Lord of lords, the great God, mighty and awesome, who shows no partiality and accepts no bribes' – and introduces a second aspect of God's greatness. Not only is he the God of cosmic ownership, he is the God of cosmic sovereignty. God's covenant sovereignty over his people has been acknowledged: Yahweh is our God and we must have no others. But this same God is also sovereign over all the nations and all the earth. He not only owns the world; he runs it. Two things are involved in this.

An impartial God

First, the end of 10:17 declares that God's sovereignty is exercised in justice. He does not show partiality or accept bribes. He is not the best God we can buy; he is a God who is independent, holy and impartial, who exercises his sovereignty in justice among the nations.

We might be tempted to think there is a contradiction between saying God is impartial (in 10:16) and that he chose and loved Israel (in 10:15). However we understand the nature of God's electing love for his people, it should not be interpreted as favouritism. In these verses his impartiality is set alongside his love for Israel and his universal sovereignty. It is another tragedy of Christian theology that the doctrine of election has sometimes been turned into a privilege for the favoured few rather than an awesome responsibility – that God has called us to his service for the sake of the other nations. Verse 15's affirmation of God's love for Israel is bounded on one side by the affirmation that God is the owner of all the earth, and on the other side by the affirmation that God does not show partiality.

Only one sovereign Lord

Secondly, notice that 'God is God of gods and Lord of lords' is a polemical statement. It is contradicting the notion that any other gods or lords might have any real sovereignty in the world.

The world in which the Israelites lived was characterized by what we would now call 'religious pluralism'. It was awash with different national gods, nature gods, and all manner of cults and idolatries. Moses was aware of this. And so a statement like the one quoted is intentionally loaded. He is saying that Yahweh, the God of Israel, is a supreme God over all other nations and all other gods and lords, whoever they may be.

This is affirmed in a specific historical context in the book of Jeremiah. In Jeremiah 27, an international diplomatic conference was taking place in Jerusalem to try to solve the problems of the Near East. The ambassadors of the surrounding countries, each with its own culture and gods, had come to Jerusalem at the invitation of King Zedekiah, in order to form a defensive alliance against Babylon. God told Jeremiah to gatecrash that conference with a great ox yoke on his shoulders and tell the ambassadors,

This is what the LORD Almighty, the God of Israel says: 'Tell this to your masters: With my great power and outstretched arm I made the earth and its people and the animals that are on it, and I give it to anyone I please. Now I will hand all your countries over to my servant Nebuchadnezzar king of Babylon' (Jeremiah 27:4-6).

To speak thus to all these people with their own gods and their own ideas of religion and sovereignty was, to say the least, not very diplomatic. It was an expression of Yahweh's universal sovereignty, contrary to the religious pluralism of the time.

We have already seen that the uniqueness of Jesus in the New Testament is founded upon the uniqueness of Yahweh in the Old Testament. In Revelation 17 we see the sovereignty of Yahweh applied to the sovereignty of Jesus: '. . . the Lamb will overcome [his enemies] because he is Lord of lords and King of kings – and with him will be his called, chosen and faithful followers' (Revelation 17:14). And in Revelation 19: 'On his robe and on his thigh he has this name written: KING OF KINGS AND LORD OF LORDS' (19:16). Paul expresses it in the familiar words of Colossians 1:15–17:

> He is the image of the invisible God, the firstborn over all creation. For by him all things were created: things in heaven and on earth, visible and invisible, whether thrones or powers or rulers or authorities; all things were created by him and for him. He is before all things, and in him all things hold together.

The exaltation of Christ is based upon the exaltation of Yahweh, the God of Israel. We need to see the unity of the Bible in these great affirmations of Old and New Testaments.

Love for the stranger

In Deuteronomy 10:18 comes the second surprise. What does this God of gods and Lord of lords do? 'He defends the cause of the fatherless and the widow, and loves the alien, giving him food and clothing.'

This is much at odds with the way Israel's neighbours in the ancient Near East perceived their own gods. Marduk, the god of Babylon, was ascribed greatness in language similar to the language celebrating Yahweh's greatness. Other gods too were exalted and worshipped as great gods. But they were great gods who upheld the power of the powerful. They gave their patronage to the kings and nobles. It was human authorities who basked in the glory of these gods. But Yahweh, the God of Israel, did not conform to this image of what gods should be like. He owns the world, runs the world, but when he is doing what he most wants to do, he is to be found among the poor, the weak and the marginalized, those without home or family or friends.

This is the surprising nature of the God of the Bible. The power of the God of gods who owns the heavens is funnelled down to the homeless, the stranger, the needy. We find something similar in Isaiah 40, where verses 12–26 describe the greatness, power and majesty of God as Creator, concluding in 40:28, 'Do you not know? Have you not heard? The LORD is the everlasting God, the Creator of the ends of the earth.' That is who he is. Yet, 'He gives strength to the weary and increases the power of the weak' (40:29). What a contrast to the gods of the ancient world, who gave power to the powerful and strengthened the already strong.

Particularly precious in Deuteronomy 10:18 is that God's love for the alien is singled out. It is an aspect of God's impartiality that he loves those who are marginalized, and feeds and clothes them. That is exactly what Deuteronomy 8 tells us God did for Israel in the wilderness. He fed them, clothed them and kept them alive, because he is the God who loves the alien.

And you shall love

If we want to imitate God, what are we to do? Verse 19 is very explicit. If God loves the orphan, the widow, the stranger, then we also are to love them. Perhaps this is what Moses had in mind when he said we should walk in all God's ways. Someone might have asked what it means to walk in the ways of the Lord, assuming that you do sincerely want to love and serve the Lord. Here Moses tells us that the way of the Lord is to love the stranger, to feed the hungry, to clothe the naked, to care for the distressed, the homeless, the orphan and the widow. Those are the ways we are to imitate God.

The precise expression 'And you shall love'

occurs only five times in the Old Testament in the Hebrew. Twice it refers to God: 'And you shall love the LORD your God.' The third instance is in Leviticus 19:18: literally, 'you shall love your neighbour as yourself.' And in Leviticus 19:34 and here in Deuteronomy 10 we have, literally, 'And you shall love the alien as yourself.' The love that we show, to be like the love of God, should not just be love for those we like to think of as our neighbours. As Jesus pointed out in the parable of the good Samaritan, our neighbour is the alien, the stranger, the Jew from the Samaritan's point of view. Moses skips right to the bottom of the pile. If you really want to walk in the way of the Lord, then you will love those who have the deepest need of your love, those otherwise excluded from the experience of love.

This practical, compassionate love for the needy is precisely the way that Jesus defined a true response to him. It is also how James defines religion that is true and acceptable to God: to care for the needy, particularly widows (James 1:27). These are the terms in both the Old and New Testaments in which the genuineness of our response to God is to be measured.

Something that disturbs me in contemporary

Christianity is that there are people who rightly want to campaign on certain moral issues, especially in the area of sexual morality, and yet seem to care less for some of the horrendous realities of our society: the plight of the homeless, the poor, the marginalized, of refugees, immigrants and asylum seekers. It is encouraging that there are Christians among those who have taken up the cause of imprisoned asylum seekers. The Bible never implies that the poor and needy are without sin, but it does say that we should take up their case and see that they are given justice.

Let our hearts beat with the love of God. Let our passion spring from the character of God, the God who owns and runs the world, who in his love and mercy chose us and brought us to himself, so that we may bring the compassion of our Lord Jesus Christ to our needy world. Thus shall we do what the Lord our God asks of us: to fear him, to walk in his ways, to love him, to serve him, and to keep his commandments.